ASEAN+3 Multi-Currency Bond Issuance Framework Implementation Guidelines for the Philippines

FEBRUARY 2020

ASIAN DEVELOPMENT BANK

ADB

Notes:
ADB recognizes "Brunei" as Brunei Darussalam and "Hong Kong" as Hong Kong, China.

In this report, international standards for naming conventions—International Organization for Standardization (ISO) 3166 for economy codes and ISO 4217 for currency codes—are used to reflect the discussions of the ASEAN+3 Bond Market Forum to promote and support implementation of international standards in financial transactions in the region. ASEAN+3 comprises the Association of Southeast Asian Nations (ASEAN) plus the People's Republic of China, Japan, and the Republic of Korea.

The economies of ASEAN+3 as defined in ISO 3166 include Brunei Darussalam (BN; BRN); Cambodia (KH; KHM); the People's Republic of China (CN; CHN); Hong Kong, China (HK; HKG); Indonesia (ID; IDN); Japan (JP; JPN); the Republic of Korea (KR; KOR); the Lao People's Democratic Republic (LA; LAO); Malaysia (MY; MYS); Myanmar (MM; MMR); the Philippines (PH; PHL); Singapore (SG; SGP); Thailand (TH; THA); and Viet Nam (VN; VNM).

The currencies of ASEAN+3 as defined in ISO 4217 include the Brunei dollar (BND), Cambodian riel (KHR), Chinese renminbi (CNY), Hong Kong dollar (HKD), Indonesian rupiah (IDR), Japanese yen (JPY), Korean won (KRW), Lao kip (LAK), Malaysian ringgit (MYR), Myanmar kyat (MMK), Philippine peso (PHP), Singapore dollar (SGD), Thai baht (THB), and Vietnamese dong (VND).

Contents

Tables and Figures

Tables

Figures

Foreword

The ASEAN+3 Bond Market Forum (ABMF) proposed the ASEAN+3 Multi-Currency Bond Issuance Framework (AMBIF) in 2014. The following year, the AMBIF's definition, purpose, and underlying practices were published.

The objective of AMBIF is to enable issuers in the Association of Southeast Asian Nations Plus Three (ASEAN+3) to issue bonds, notes, or *sukuk* (Islamic bonds) in the professional market or market segment of any participating economy in a comparable manner, using the same or similar practices and a standardized approach to disclosure. This, in turn, allows for a streamlined approval process (where required), lower costs, and faster time-to-market. The underlying incentive of AMBIF, pursuant to the original mandate of ABMF, was to improve intra-regional bond transactions in ASEAN+3.

AMBIF itself does not change a market's legal or regulatory framework. Instead, AMBIF employs the existing characteristics of each economy's professional bond market by using those features comparable to the AMBIF Elements, which are a normalized set of underlying requirements for eligible issuances. Issuer and investor criteria, place of issuance, and currency considerations are part of the AMBIF Elements. One key element is the creation and use of the Single Submission Form as the single common document for information disclosure across all AMBIF markets.

The AMBIF Implementation Guidelines for each participating market are provided to review the AMBIF Elements and detail the corresponding features of the participating market in relation to each element. Following the proven approach for output created by ABMF, the AMBIF Implementation Guidelines have been reviewed and their contents approved by each market's respective regulatory authorities so that interested parties, particularly issuers and their service providers, can pursue further issuances under AMBIF with ease and certainty.

This document explains the AMBIF Elements; puts into perspective the corresponding features of the professional Philippine bond market; highlights market characteristics that are significant for issuers and investors; and reviews the regulatory processes required for different types of issuances of debt securities, including for both resident and nonresident issuers and for different issuer types, as may be applicable.

Yasuyuki Sawada
Chief Economist and Director General
Economic Research and Regional Cooperation Department

Acknowledgments

The AMBIF Implementation Guidelines for the Philippines were first published in 2015 as part of the Phase 2 Report of the ASEAN+3 Bond Market Forum (ABMF).[1] Across the region, domestic bond markets, including the bond market in the Philippines, have experienced tremendous development over the past 5 years. Now in Phase 3, ABMF would like to share, in the public domain, information on these developments by publishing an update to the AMBIF Implementation Guidelines for the Philippines as a standalone document, with a particular focus on market features that represent, or influence, AMBIF Elements in the Philippines.

The ASEAN+3 Bond Market Forum (ABMF) Sub-Forum 1 team comprising Satoru Yamadera, Principal Financial Sector Specialist, Economic Research and Regional Cooperation Department (ERCD), Asian Development Bank (ADB); Kosintr Puongsophol, Financial Sector Specialist, ERCD, ADB; and ADB consultants Shigehito Inukai and Matthias Schmidt would like to stress the significance and magnitude of the contributions made by ABMF national members and experts for the Philippines, including the Bangko Sentral ng Pilipinas, Bankers Association of the Philippines, Philippine Dealing & Exchange Corporation, and Securities and Exchange Commission of the Philippines. These policy bodies, regulatory authorities, and market institutions generously gave their time for market visit meetings, discussions, and follow-up. They have also reviewed and provided inputs on the draft AMBIF Implementation Guidelines for the Philippines over the course of ABMF Phase 3.

No part of this report represents the official views or opinions of any institution that participated in this activity as an ABMF member, observer, or expert. The ABMF Sub-Forum 1 team bears sole responsibility for the contents of this report.

ASEAN+3 Bond Market Forum

---

[1] ASEAN+3 refers to the 10 members of the Association of Southeast Asian Nations (ASEAN) plus the People's Republic of China, Japan, and the Republic of Korea.

Abbreviations

ABMF	ASEAN+3 Bond Market Forum
ADB	Asian Development Bank
AMBIF	ASEAN+3 Multi-Currency Bond Issuance Framework
ASEAN	Association of Southeast Asian Nations
ASEAN+3	Association of Southeast Asian Nations plus the People's Republic of China, Japan, and the Republic of Korea
BSP	Bangko Sentral ng Pilipinas
CNH	offshore Chinese renminbi
CRA	credit rating agency
FCY	foreign currency
FX	foreign exchange
IRR	Implementing Rules and Regulations
LCY	local currency
MORB	Manual of Regulations for Banks
MORNBFI	Manual of Regulations for Non-Bank Financial Institutions
MTN	medium-term note
OTC	over-the-counter
PDEx	Philippine Dealing & Exchange Corp.
PDTC	Philippine Depository & Trust Corp.
QB	Qualified Buyer
SEC	Securities and Exchange Commission
SF1	Sub-Forum 1 of ABMF
SRC	Securities Regulation Code
SSF	Single Submission Form

AMBIF Elements in the Philippines

This chapter describes the key features of the ASEAN+3 Multi-Currency Bond Issuance Framework (AMBIF), also known as the AMBIF Elements, and puts into perspective the equivalent features of the domestic professional bond market in the Philippines.

A.   Summary of AMBIF Elements

The bond market in the Philippines features many of the attributes of a professional market in the context of AMBIF, including the well-defined Qualified Buyers and Qualified Securities exemptions from full disclosure and related regulatory processes, and from existing registration and listing processes. Issuances to Qualified Buyers, which are generally referred to as QB bonds, together with enrollment on the Philippine Dealing & Exchange Corp. (PDEx), are presently deemed to best represent the intentions of the AMBIF Elements.

As a Securities and Exchange Commission (SEC)-registered exchange and SEC-authorized over-the-counter (OTC) market operator, PDEx operates the organized secondary market for the trading of fixed-income securities, which includes both government securities and corporate bonds and notes.

Table 1 identifies the features and practices of the domestic corporate bond market in the Philippines that directly correspond or are equivalent to the AMBIF Elements.

Table 1: AMBIF Elements and Equivalent Features in the Philippines

AMBIF Element	Description	Equivalent in the Philippines
Domestic Settlement	Securities are settled at a national CSD in each ASEAN+3 market.	PDTC is the depository and place of settlement for all eligible bonds and notes.
Harmonized Documents for Submission (Single Submission Form)	There is a common approach to submitting information as input to regulatory process(es) where approval or consent is required; appropriate disclosure information, based on an ADRB recommendation, needs to be included.	The Single Submission Form is acceptable but additional information and document(s) may be requested during the evaluation process, as necessary.

Registration or Profile Listing in ASEAN+3 (Place of Continuous Disclosure)	Information on bonds, notes, and issuer needs to be disclosed continuously in the relevant ASEAN+3 market. A registration or listing authority function is required to ensure continuous and quality disclosure.	Enrollment of bonds or notes on the PDEx Qualified Board is required, including continuous disclosure obligation by the sponsor under the Listing and Enrollment Rules; reference pricing for traded instruments is available.
Currency	Bonds or notes are denominated in one of the currencies normally used for issuances in the domestic bond market of an ASEAN+3 member.	Philippine pesos and US dollars
Scope of Issuers	Resident of an ASEAN+3 member	Philippine and nonresident regional issuers, in accordance with BSP regulatory processes based on type of issuer, residency, and currency of denomination
Scope of Investors	Professional investors defined in accordance with the applicable laws, regulations, or market practice in each market in ASEAN+3	QB concept—as per the Securities Regulation Code and provisions in the MORFXT, as may be applicable—which includes foreign institutional investors

ADRB = AMBIF Documentation Recommendation Board; AMBIF = ASEAN+3 Multi-Currency Bond Issuance Framework; ASEAN+3 = Association of Southeast Asian Nations plus the People's Republic of China, Japan, and the Republic of Korea; BSP = Bangko Sentral ng Pilipinas; CSD = central securities depository; MORFXT = Manual of Regulations for Foreign Exchange Transactions; PDEx = Philippine Dealing & Exchange Corp.; PDTC = Philippine Depository & Trust Corp.; QB = Qualified Buyer; SEC = Securities and Exchange Commission; US = United States.
Source: ABMF SF1.

B.   Description of AMBIF Elements and Equivalent Features in the Philippines

The market features in the Philippines that are comparable to the AMBIF Elements listed in Table 1 are explained in this section in greater detail.

1.   Domestic Settlement

ASEAN+3 Multi-Currency Bond Issuance Framework

AMBIF is aimed at supporting the domestic bond markets of ASEAN+3 member economies. To be recognized as a domestic bond, an AMBIF bond or note needs to be settled at the designated central securities depository. Hence, domestic settlement is a key feature of an AMBIF bond.

Equivalent Features in the Philippines

The Philippine Depository & Trust Corp. (PDTC) is the designated central depository for equities and corporate bonds and notes. With the exception of a number of corporate notes that are not listed on PDEx, PDTC settles and provides safekeeping for all fixed-income instruments traded on PDEx. Both entities are subsidiaries of the Philippine Dealing System Holdings Corp.

2. Harmonized Documents for Submission (Single Submission Form)

ASEAN+3 Multi-Currency Bond Issuance Framework

Based on the review of actual offering circulars, information memoranda, and program information formats in ASEAN+3, it was recognized that most information was similar or comparable. Hence, a Single Submission Form (SSF)—a single format in English that can be applied to all of the relevant regulatory processes for bond or note issuance in each participating ASEAN+3 market—was proposed. The information contained in the SSF has been normalized based on the prevailing regulations in each participating market and therefore can be accepted by all relevant regulatory authorities and market institutions for their respective approvals or consent in anticipation of an AMBIF bond or note issuance.

Equivalent Features in the Philippines

In the Philippines, regulatory authorities and market institutions accept the SSF, though this does not preclude the possibility of additional information being submitted to the authorities if deemed necessary.[1] At the time of writing, the SSF was in the process of being updated to incorporate additional information required under the PDEx Rules.

Effective 9 November 2015, the filing of a Notice of Exempt Transaction (SEC Form 10.1) with the SEC is no longer required when a resident corporate issuer wants to issue bonds or notes to professional investors (Qualified Buyer issuances) in the Philippines. As a result, the pilot AMBIF issuance in the Philippines in October 2018 made use of the SSF as the key disclosure document to Qualified Investors and was submitted as a matter of record to the BSP.

However, corporate issuers still have the option to request for a Confirmation of Exempt Transaction from the SEC (see also Chapter III.D). This option was already available to issuers in the previous Implementing Rules and Regulations (IRR) of the Securities Regulation Code (SRC).

The use of English is prescribed in BSP and SEC regulations, including the provisions related to PDEx.

3. Registration or Profile Listing in ASEAN+3 (Place of Continuous Disclosure)

ASEAN+3 Multi-Currency Bond Issuance Framework

Information on the issuer and the bond or note needs to be disclosed continuously in ASEAN+3 markets. A registration or listing authority function to ensure continuous disclosure is required. This will also ensure the quality of information disclosure and help create a transparent, well-organized market for AMBIF issuances that is differentiated from ordinary private placements or exempt offers for which information is often neither available nor guaranteed. Owing to this important feature, an AMBIF secondary market is expected to emerge as the number of issuances increase.

---

[1] For the AMBIF pilot issuance in the Philippines, the SSF was accepted by PDEx for its application for enrollment. SEC and BSP approval was not necessary at the time.

A profile listing is a listing without trading. The objective of a profile listing is to make a bond or note visible and to provide more information to investors via a recognized listing place, particularly those investors with more restrictive mandates such as mutual and pension funds. A profile listing at a designated listing place can ensure the flow of continuous disclosure information and possibly even reference pricing in some markets.

Equivalent Features in the Philippines

In the Philippines, the listing or enrollment of a bond or note on PDEx covers listing and enrollment, as well as trading processes and practices, for debt instruments. According to the PDEx Listing and Enrollment Rules (7.2.1), a listing or enrollment is possible for debt instruments issued by either resident or nonresident issuers. A listing or enrollment of a note issuance program, such as a medium-term note (MTN) program, is principally possible. PDEx is in the process of implementing a framework for bank issuances (see Chapter III.F for details).

The listing or enrollment of bonds or commercial paper by banks or quasi-banks registered in the Philippines is subject to the PDEx Guidelines for Listing or Enrollment of Bank-Issued Bonds and Commercial Paper, as approved by the SEC and pursuant to BSP Circular No. 1010 (2018) on Additional Requirements for the Issuance of Bonds and Commercial Paper, which became effective on 15 October 2018. Under the BSP circular, such bonds and commercial paper are required to be listed or enrolled on an organized securities market approved by the SEC; PDEx is such a market. More details on the relevance of the direct applicability of the guidelines and the underlying BSP circular can be found in Chapter III.

A listing of a bond or note is for instruments open to all investors and needs to be initiated by the issuer. In contrast, an enrollment is for bonds and notes aimed at Qualified Buyers (professional investors), or those considered Restricted Securities, and may be initiated by the issuer or a trading participant.[2] The party who enrolls a bond or note on PDEx, also referred to as the sponsor, is responsible for the disclosure of material information as stipulated in the PDEx Listing and Enrollment Rules. A listing or enrollment on PDEx requires the appointment of a facility agent or trustee by the issuer. In the event of the issuer being a bank or quasi-bank, the issuer will need to appoint at least one market maker; the issuing bank or quasi-bank must have an issuer or issue credit rating provided by a credit rating agency (CRA) duly accredited by the BSP.

A listing or enrollment of a bond or note on PDEx does not automatically require trading. However, should the issuer or sponsor of a bond or note enrolled on PDEx wish to trade the instrument, all trades must be done on PDEx. According to the Rules Governing the Over-the-Counter Market (OTC Rules) issued by the SEC in 2006, all OTC trading of debt instruments issued in the Philippines needs to occur in an SEC-authorized marketplace. PDEx is such an authorized marketplace. Hence, the listing or enrollment is a necessary step to ultimately trade a bond or note in the OTC market in the Philippines.

At the same time, PDEx also principally offers the feature of profile listing in the form of the so-called Qualified Board, which takes its name from its designation to enroll (by the issuer) only bonds or notes issued to professional investors, or Restricted Securities.

---

[2] Restricted Securities refer to debt securities that are issued by a financial institution without a quasi-banking license as an Exempt Transaction under Section 10.1 (l) of the SRC. Restricted Securities are required to not exceed a maximum of 19 investors, which is referred to as the "19-lender limit," during their tenor. Please see Chapter III for more details.

Under the OTC Rules, the SEC conferred listing authority functions on PDEx. The PDEx Listing and Enrollment Rules compel the continuous disclosure of material information from issuers or sponsors of a bond or note listed or enrolled on PDEx. PDEx also publishes bond pricing information based on actual traded prices that have to be captured by deal parties within 1 minute of deal closure and reported in the Central Trade Reporting System within 15 minutes, as provided under Section 16 of the OTC Rules.

In addition, or as an alternative, the issuer may opt for a profile listing in another regional market in order to achieve listing status closer to an intended investor universe. This may be a consideration, particularly if a bond or note issued in the Philippines will be marketed and offered to professional investors in other ASEAN+3 economies. In such cases, the professional investor would be able to obtain continuous disclosure information via the listing place and/or that market's mechanisms for information dissemination.

4. Currency

ASEAN+3 Multi-Currency Bond Issuance Framework

In the context of AMBIF, the denomination of a bond or note is expected to be the currency normally issued in the domestic bond markets of ASEAN+3 (i.e., the local currency of that particular market). This does not exclude the possibility of issuing in other currencies if market practice regularly supports these other currencies and if cash-clearing capabilities exist. At present, the United States (US) dollar (ISO code: USD), Japanese yen (ISO code: JPY), and offshore Chinese renminbi (ISO code: CNH) are the other currencies most commonly in use in ASEAN+3 markets.

Equivalent Features in the Philippines

In addition to settlement for bonds and notes issued in Philippine pesos, PDTC can also settle bonds and notes denominated in US dollars that are registered in the Philippines and listed on PDEx, as the Philippines features a domestic US dollar clearing system. In recent years, PDEx has listed a number of USD-denominated bonds issued by the Government of the Philippines.

5. Scope of Issuers

ASEAN+3 Multi-Currency Bond Issuance Framework

As AMBIF aims to support the development of domestic bond and note markets in the region and promote the intra-regional recycling of funds, an issuer must be a resident of ASEAN+3.

Equivalent Features in the Philippines

The SEC does not differentiate between resident and nonresident issuers. However, nonresident issuers wishing to use the proceeds from a PHP-denominated bond or note issued in a foreign currency (FCY) may require a policy decision by the SEC.

As for the purview of the BSP, the rules applied to the onshore issuance of bonds or notes may vary depending on whether the issuer is a resident or nonresident, and whether the bonds or notes are denominated in Philippine pesos or another currency. In addition, if the issuer is a financial institution, other prudential considerations may apply (see also Chapter III).

For resident nonfinancial institution issuers, no prior BSP approval is required for the onshore issuance of bonds, notes, and other similar instruments (not resembling in nature a foreign loan) that are denominated in pesos. For resident financial institutions, the issuance of PHP-denominated bonds and notes is allowed, subject to regulations governing the borrowing of banks and quasi-banks under the provisions of the new Manual of Regulations for Banks (MORB) and the Manual of Regulations for Non-Bank Financial Institutions (MORNBFI), respectively, including those amended via BSP Circular No. 1010 (2018) (see Chapter III). However, the issuance of unsecured subordinated debt instruments that will be counted as regulatory capital by banks and quasi-banks is subject to BSP approval.

Similarly, no prior BSP approval is required for onshore issuances by residents (both financial and nonfinancial institutions) of bonds or notes (not resembling in nature a foreign loan) that are denominated in a foreign currency.[3] On the other hand, prior BSP approval is required for issuances by residents of bonds, notes, and other similar instruments with public sector involvement either as an issuer or borrower, or as a guarantor.[4]

For nonresident issuers, the onshore issuance of bonds, notes, and similar instruments (regardless of the currency of denomination) requires BSP approval before execution of the transaction. Table 2 gives an overview of these approval criteria for easy reference.

Table 2: Overview of BSP Approvals for Issuance of Bonds and Notes by Issuer Type

Issuer	Currency of Bond or Note Issuance	
	Philippine Peso	Foreign Currency
Resident nonfinancial institution[a]	No prior BSP approval is required (for issuances not resembling in nature a foreign loan). However, a Monetary Board opinion is required for government domestic borrowing.[b]	
Resident financial institution[a]	1. Issuance is subject to regulations on the borrowing of banks and quasi-banks under the Manual of Regulations for Banks. 2. Issuance of unsecured subordinated debt instruments that shall be counted as regulatory capital by banks or quasi-banks is subject to BSP approval.	
Nonresident nonfinancial institution	Subject to BSP approval prior to execution of transaction	
Nonresident financial institution		

BSP = Bangko Sentral ng Pilipinas.
Note: At present, there were no distinctions between approvals for issuances in either Philippine pesos or a foreign currency; however, this could eventually change.
[a] Prior BSP approval is required for resident issuances of bonds, notes, and other similar instruments (not resembling in nature a foreign loan) with public sector involvement either as an issuer or borrower, or as a guarantor.
[b] Pursuant to Section 123 of Republic Act No. 7653 (as amended).
Source: BSP.

---

[3] The corresponding provisions are contained in Section 22 of the Manual of Regulations for Foreign Exchange Transactions (as amended by BSP Circular No. 1030 dated 5 February 2019), which is also known as the Foreign Exchange Manual.
[4] Sections 22, 23, 24, and 31.3 of the Manual of Regulations for Foreign Exchange Transactions (as amended by BSP Circular No. 1030 dated 5 February 2019).

Both resident and nonresident issuers may list or enroll their debt instruments aimed at Qualified Buyers on PDEx, depending on the SEC framework. Pursuant to prescriptions in BSP Circular No. 1010 (2018), banks and quasi-banks must enroll their debt securities on PDEx. For more details on PDEx and the regulatory processes of the BSP and SEC, please refer to Chapters II and III, respectively.

6. Scope of Investors

ASEAN+3 Multi-Currency Bond Issuance Framework

Professional investors are defined in accordance with regulations and/or market practice in each market in ASEAN+3. Some jurisdictions may have a clear definition of professional investors, while other jurisdictions may need to establish the concept through agreements.

Professional investors are institutions defined by law and licensed or otherwise registered with regulators by law in their economy of domicile and, hence, are subject to governance and inspection based on securities market and/or prudential regulations. Most of them are also subject to oversight and professional conduct and best practice rules by a self-regulatory organization such as an exchange or a market association.

Equivalent Features in the Philippines

Section 10.1 of the SRC describes professional investors as Qualified Buyers. Concessions on disclosure and obligations under the Qualified Buyer concept are prescribed in this section. At present, the issuance of bonds or notes to Qualified Buyers, which are generally referred to as QB bonds, constitutes the professional bond market in the Philippines. The descriptions of regulatory processes included in Chapter III are for corporate QB bond issuances only.

The SRC deals with so-called Exempt Transactions—circumstances under which concessions from the full disclosure and approval processes of the SEC are available. Section 10.1 (l) prescribes exemptions from full disclosure and the related approval process when issuing bonds or notes to the following institutions, thereby decreeing them as professional investors:

  i.   banks,
  ii.   registered investment houses,
  iii. insurance companies,
  iv.   pension funds or retirement schemes,
  v.   investment companies, and
  vi.   other institutions or individuals as determined by the SEC.[5]

SEC Memorandum Circular No. 10 (2018) provided that unit investment trust funds and funds established and covered by a trust or investment management agreement under a discretionary arrangement shall be considered a Qualified Buyer.[6] Funds established and covered by a trust or investment management agreement under a nondiscretionary arrangement shall be considered a Qualified Buyer provided that it has complied with the conditions, including the financial capacity requirement, specified in 2015 in SRC Rule 10.1.11.1 for natural persons and SRC Rule 10.1.11.2 for juridical persons.

---

[5] SRC Rule 10.1.1 provides the financial capacity and sophistication requirements for a Qualified Buyer.
[6] SEC Memorandum Circular No. 10 (2018) on Rules and Regulations on Determination of Trust Fund as a Qualified Buyer is available at http://www.sec.gov.ph/wp-content/uploads/2018/08/2018MCNo10.pdf.

In order to be considered a Qualified Buyer, eligible institutions must register with a registrar authorized by the SEC; the formal title is Registrar of Qualified Institutional and Individual Buyers. Pursuant to SRC Rule 39.1.4.1, the institutions eligible to be registrars include

   i.   banks, with respect to their registration as a broker–dealer, Government Securities Eligible Dealers, Government Securities Brokers, and/or underwriters of securities;
   ii. brokers;
   iii. dealers;
   iv. investment houses;
   v.   investment company advisers; and
   vi. issuer companies with respect to offerings of their own securities.

The act of registration with an authorized registrar fulfills the assessment and confirmation of the eligibility of a Qualified Buyer to invest in QB bonds. If the registration is successful, the registrar will issue a certificate of registration to the Qualified Buyer, which is valid for 3 years from the date of registration. A registrar is required to maintain a registry book and provide an annual report to the SEC on the number of Qualified Buyers in its registry and selected additional information as prescribed in SRC Rule 39.1.4.4.7.

In practice, the registration does not require an extra step in the investment process; Qualified Buyers are typically—if not previously—registered with the underwriter from which they intend to buy QB bonds during the solicitation or book-building process.

There is no distinction in the SRC, or in the related IRR, between domestic and foreign professional investors.

For investments in bonds or notes issued onshore, the following BSP rules shall apply:

   i.   In cases of investments in PHP-denominated bonds and notes issued by residents:
         a. investments by residents may be done without BSP approval; and
         b. investments by nonresidents may be done without prior BSP approval, subject to registration only if the foreign exchange (FX) to service repatriation of capital and related earnings will be sourced from the Philippine banking system.

   ii. In cases of investments in PHP-denominated bonds and notes issued by nonresidents:
         a. investments by residents may be done without BSP approval; and
         b. investments by nonresidents may be done without prior BSP approval, subject to registration only if the FX to service repatriation of capital and related earnings will be sourced from the Philippine banking system.

   iii. In cases of investments in FCY-denominated bonds and notes issued by residents:
         a. investments by residents may be done without BSP approval; and
         b. investments by nonresidents may be done without prior BSP approval, but sourcing of the FX from the Philippine banking system by a resident issuer is subject to documentation (for bonds and notes [not resembling in nature a foreign loan] or registration [for bonds and notes resembling in nature a foreign loan).

iv.   In cases of investments in FCY-denominated bonds and notes issued onshore by nonresidents:

    a. investments by residents may be done without prior BSP approval, subject to notification to the BSP only if the investment exceeds the USD60 million annual threshold per investor; the FX to service redemption and coupon payments cannot be sourced from the Philippine banking system by a nonresident issuer; and

    b. investments by nonresidents may be done without BSP approval, but the FX to service the redemption and coupon payments cannot be sourced from the Philippine banking system by a nonresident issuer.

Table 3 gives an overview of the abovementioned approval criteria for investment in bonds and notes issued in the Philippines.

Table 3: Overview of BSP Approvals for Investment in Bonds and Notes

Investor	Issuer	
	Resident	**Nonresident**
PHP-Denominated Bonds and Notes		
Resident	Allowed	Allowed
Nonresident	Allowed, subject to registration only if the FX to service repatriation of capital and related earnings will be sourced from the Philippine banking system	Allowed, subject to registration only if the FX to service repatriation of capital and related earnings will be sourced from the Philippine banking system
FCY-Denominated Bonds and Notes		
Resident	Allowed	Allowed, subject to notification to BSP and documentation only if the investment exceeds the USD60 million annual threshold per investor; the FX to service redemption and coupon payments cannot be sourced from the Philippine banking system
Nonresident	Allowed, but sourcing of the FX from the Philippine banking system by resident issuers is subject to documentation (for bonds and notes not resembling in nature a foreign loan) or registration (for bonds and notes resembling in nature a foreign loan)	Allowed, but the FX to service redemption and coupon payments by nonresident issuers cannot be sourced from the Philippine banking system

FCY = foreign currency, FX = foreign exchange, PHP = Philippine peso, USD = United States dollar.
Source: Bangko Sentral ng Pilipinas.

II

AMBIF Bond and Note Issuance: Relevant Features in the Philippines

In addition to market features corresponding to the AMBIF Elements, a number of general Philippine market features for bond and note issuance to professional investors (Qualified Buyers) need to be considered by market participants. These features are described in this chapter.

In choosing a location to issue bonds, cost is a major consideration. While the AMBIF Implementation Guidelines only refer to applicable fees and charges arising from bond and note issuance under AMBIF, the ASEAN+3 Bond Market Guide for the Philippines contains a comprehensive chapter with descriptions of the typical cost factors such as registration fees, listing fees, enrollment fees, documentary stamp taxes, and taxes on interest income. The ASEAN+3 Bond Market Guide for the Philippines also contains information on relevant taxation for debt securities.

A.   Governing Law and Jurisdiction

Governing law and the jurisdiction for specific service provisions in relation to a bond or note issuance may have some relevance in the context of AMBIF. Potential issuers may consider issuing under the laws or jurisdiction of an economy or market other than the place of issuance. The choice of governing law or the contractual preferences of stakeholders can affect accessibility to a specific investor universe that may otherwise not be accessible if a bond or note were issued under the laws of the place of issuance. However, provisions related to bond or note issuance and settlement must be governed by the laws and regulations of the place of issuance since an AMBIF bond is a domestic bond.

The civil code of the Philippines permits the use of governing law or jurisdictions other than the Philippines in contracts, provided that such provisions do not contravene existing Philippine law.

Should the parties involved in a bond or note issuance choose to use Philippine law, the jurisdiction of the issuance would fall to Philippine courts by default. If anything other than Philippine law is chosen as the governing law in the transaction documents, the parties thereto may choose the specific jurisdiction of a court in which disputes will be adjudicated.

In the case of issuance of PHP-denominated bonds or notes in the Philippines, even in cases when contract parties choose a governing law other than Philippine law for the contract, it is expected that Philippine law would prevail as the law specific to issuance- and settlement-related matters.

Notwithstanding the above, Philippine courts and courts of other jurisdictions may have jurisdiction over disputes arising in relation to such bond issuances, to the extent permitted by Philippine or other relevant laws.

In any case, the actual use of governing laws or jurisdictions other than those of the Philippines may be subject to clarification or legal advice from a qualified law firm, as may be necessary.

B.   Language of Documentation and Disclosure Items

It is envisaged that most ASEAN+3 markets participating in AMBIF will accept the use of a common document in English. However, some markets may require the submission of approval-related information in their prescribed format and in the local language. In such cases, concessions from the regulatory authorities for a submission of required information in English—in addition to the local language and formats—may be sought.

In the Philippines, an English translation shall be used in all documentation with regard to the issuance of bonds or notes.

C.   Credit Rating

Bonds and notes to be listed or enrolled on PDEx require a credit rating in line with the credit rating requirements stipulated by the SEC and the BSP. This includes bank-issued bonds and commercial paper.

In its Memorandum Circular No. 7 released in March 2014, the SEC announced the Guidelines on the Accreditation, Operations, and Reporting of Credit Rating Agencies, which govern the two domestic CRAs—Philippine Rating Services (PhilRatings) and Credit Rating and Investors Services Philippines—and clarify the acceptance of credit ratings from international CRAs. The guidelines on accreditation are now included in SRC Rule 39.1.5.

BSP-supervised financial institutions can source capital through the issuance of "unsecured subordinated debt," which can be used as Tier 2 capital. Issuing this type of debt to the public requires a rating from a recognized CRA.

PhilRatings was the first domestic CRA to be recognized by the BSP, based on minimum eligibility criteria for bank supervisory purposes. The BSP also recognizes the credit ratings of internationally accepted CRAs—such as Fitch Ratings, Moody's, and Standard & Poor's, as well as Fitch Singapore—for bank supervisory purposes. PDEx accepts the credit rating of the issuer or issue from a CRA duly recognized by the applicable regulatory authorities.

Unrated bonds and notes are possible under present regulations and may be listed on the PDEx Qualified Board. However, it has been observed that potential AMBIF investors may prefer that bonds and notes have a credit rating.

D.   Selling and Transfer Restrictions

Selling and transfer restrictions for the issuance of bonds or notes to professional investors are well defined in the identified professional market segment in the Philippines (Qualified Buyers and Qualified Securities).

Pursuant to Sections 9 and 10 of the SRC, the IRR published by the SEC prescribe a template and specific provisions on the use of that template, and define the selling and/or transfer restrictions when issuing bonds or notes to Qualified Buyers.

To further ensure the validity of an exemption claimed by an issuer under Section 10.1 of the SRC when issuing bonds or notes aimed at Qualified Buyers, the SEC also looks to the underwriter—licensed by the SEC—to observe the applicable provisions and selling and transfer restrictions under the law.

In all offer documents and related correspondence to Qualified Buyers, including the term sheet of a proposed bond or note issue, an issuer must make explicit reference to Section 10.1 (I) of the SRC and give their commitment that said offer is limited to Qualified Buyers, thereby constituting an Exempt Transaction under the law. The IRR related to Section 10.1 (1.c) of the SRC prescribe the following statement in bold face and prominent type:

> The securities being offered or sold have not been registered with the Securities and Exchange Commission under the Securities Regulation Code, any future offer or sale thereof is subject to registration requirements under the Code unless such offer or sale qualifies as an Exempt Transaction.

In addition, appropriate selling or transfer restrictions will need to be printed on the actual issued instrument, typically global or jumbo certificate(s) in bold font if certificates are to be issued. However, Philippine company law does not require the physical issuance of certificates. PDEx also requires all its listing or enrollments to be dematerialized; hence, the lack of certificates means that no explicit selling restrictions will need to be printed.

If a bond or note is listed or enrolled on PDEx, as discussed in Chapter I, the observance of applicable selling and transfer restrictions is part of the explicit warranties that issuers and participants give to PDEx when signing up. Under the premise that an exemption from registration may be impaired if enrolled securities are held by non-Qualified Buyers, a set of conventions, controls, and processes are included within the PDEx operating framework that focus on the mitigation of the risk of transfers to non-Qualified Buyers and the resolution of situations when holdings of enrolled securities have been verified to be with non-Qualified Buyers. See also section G for information on issuances to Qualified Buyers and the nature of, or available exemptions from, registration.

There is no distinction between domestic issuers and nonresident issuers with regard to selling or transfer restrictions and their observance.

E.   19-Lender Rule and Its Applications

The so-called "19-lender rule" is unique to the Philippines and refers to a borrower not being able to borrow money from more than 19 lenders unless it has secured the requisite license with the BSP, if applicable. In the context of the bond market, an issuer cannot issue its debt securities to more than 19 investors without affecting its licensing status; the number of investors must not exceed 19 at any time during the lifecycle of the debt securities. The 19-lender rule is relevant only to certain non-bank financial institutions.

Relevance for Quasi-Banking License and BSP Supervision

The 19-lender limit was originally introduced by the BSP as one of the measures to regulate the relevant activities of so-called lending companies (granting direct loans to the public) as non-bank financial institutions. Non-bank financial institutions do not have a full banking license but facilitate banking-related financial services such as investment, risk pooling, contractual savings activities, and market brokering. The coverage of the 19-lender distinction was eventually extended to financing companies—those companies engaged in, for example, leasing, factoring, and discounting—that carried out bank-like activities. The underlying objective is to regulate the activities of non-bank financial institutions performing functions similar to a bank (i.e., quasi-banking) such as deposit taking, raising funds, and consumer lending. Hence, the term "quasi-bank" can be found in BSP regulations and nomenclature. The term "non-bank quasi-bank" is also used.

Table 4: Quasi-Banking Consideration by Borrower Type

Borrower	Quasi-Banking Consideration	
	Status	Condition
Commercial company	No	Not under BSP supervision
Industrial company	No	Not under BSP supervision
Other nonfinancial company	No	Not under BSP supervision
Lending company	No	In case of normal activities under relevant regulations
	Yes	If 20 or more lenders (investors) at any one time
Financing company	No	Regular leasing, forfeiting, discounting exempt
	Yes	If 20 or more lenders (investors) at any one time

BSP = Bangko Sentral ng Pilipinas.
Source: ABMF SF1.

At present, all borrowing and debt-financing activities of lending and financing companies involving 20 or more lenders (investors) are regarded as quasi-banking (Table 4), pursuant to the so-called "Q Regulations" in the MORNBFI and, consequently, require a quasi-banking license from the BSP and are subject to BSP supervision. Under the Q Regulations, borrowing is defined as the issuance, endorsement, or acceptance of debt instruments of any kind other than deposits. Financing companies that do not require a quasi-banking license are generally supervised by the SEC and subject to the Financing Company Act, 1969, while lending companies are licensed by the municipality in which they operate and are subject to the provisions of the Lending Company Regulation Act, 2004.

The 19-lender limit has also been embedded in Section 10.1.(k) of the SRC. Potential non-bank financial institution issuers of AMBIF bonds are advised to consider the 19-lender rule carefully.

Recent Clarification of Deposit Substitutes and Impact on 19-Lender Rule

Republic Act No. 11211, which amended the New Central Bank Act (Republic Act No. 7653), also known as the BSP Charter, was signed into law on 14 February 2019. The amendment included a clarification of the definition of "deposit substitutes" that had a significant impact on the 19-lender rule.

When clarifying the phrase "obtaining funds from the public," the term "lenders," which is relevant for the rule of borrowing money from 20 or more lenders, was adjusted to not include financial intermediaries. For all intents and purposes, the constituents of the term "financial intermediaries" are eligible as Qualified Buyers. Hence, in accordance with the updated definition of deposit substitutes exempting financial intermediaries from the lender count, Qualified Buyers, as defined under Section 10.1 (I) of the SRC, that are financial intermediaries are excluded from the lender count for the purpose of the 19-lender rule.

Relevance as Criteria for Restricted Issuers and Restricted Securities

In the context of issuance and the listing or enrollment of debt securities on PDEx, Restricted Issuers are financial institutions without a quasi-banking license (hence, falling under BSP supervision) that must observe the 19-lender rule when issuing debt instruments lest they require a quasi-banking license.[8] The restriction to issue to and maintain a maximum number of 19 investors (lenders) must be observed at all times during the tenor of the debt securities, notwithstanding the exception of financial intermediaries mentioned above. Such debt securities are, consequently, also known as Restricted Securities.

Pursuant to the PDEx Guidelines for Restricted Issuers and Non-Reporting Companies, which were issued as an addendum to the PDEx Enrollment Rules in October 2018, the terms Restricted Issuers and Restricted Securities only apply to issuers that issue or sell debt securities under an Exempt Transaction pursuant to Section 10.1 (I) of the SRC or SRC Rule 10.1.3, respectively, and which are limited only to Qualified Buyers. Such debt securities are also known as QB bonds. In fact, Restricted Securities represent a subset of QB bonds.

F.   Note Issuance Program

AMBIF promotes the MTN program (or the note issuance program) format because it not only gives funding flexibility to issuers, but it also represents the most common format of bond issuance in the international bond market. This means that potential issuers as well as investors and intermediaries are likely to be familiar with the note issuance programs and related practices in ASEAN+3 markets. Hence, this would make AMBIF comparable to the relevant practices of the international bond market. At the same time, it is expected that potential issuers can benefit from reusing or adopting existing documentation and information disclosure. The SSF already supports multiple issuances.

As of August 2019, a framework for handling the listing or enrollment of bank-issued bonds issued under an "MTN-like" program had been approved by the PDEx Market Governance Board and submitted to the SEC for final approval. Since bank-issued bonds may have shorter tenors than medium-term notes, the framework was named the Bank Bond Issuance Program. The PDEx framework for listing or enrolling bank-issued bonds under this program essentially follows the same approach as for corporate bonds issued under an SEC-approved shelf registration.

While such a shelf-registration concept has been in existence for some time, it is not directly comparable to shelf-registration concepts typically practiced in other markets. The 2015 version of the SRC Rules, which represented the first major update of the original SRC Rules published in 2005, aimed to implement global and regional best practices while easing local regulations, particularly in the bond market. Among the many changes and refinements in the SRC Rules were the provisions to (i) make the

---

[8] Under the SRC and its IRR, the count for the 19-lender limit of a non-quasi-bank issuer includes all holders of securities issued by the non-quasi-bank as well as all other direct lenders such as banks.

shelf-registration of debt securities easier, including a longer issuance period and faster time-to-market; and (ii) offer the ability to pay registration fees in line with multitranche issuances rather than pay upfront for the total issuance size. However, many of these concessions for shelf-registration refer to public offers.

G. Issuance to Qualified Buyers

The typical definition of a private placement is the issuance of bonds or notes to professional investors under exemptions or concessions from full disclosure or defined regulatory processes. There is no official mention or definition of private placement in law or regulations in the Philippines.

Instead, bonds or notes aimed at Qualified Buyers (QB bonds), or those classified as Exempt Transactions under the SRC, typically fulfill the traditional expectations of a private placement in which the target group is professional investors and the issue is subject to exemption from full disclosure under applicable regulations and, in the case of the Philippines, registration with and approval from the SEC. As such, the professional bond market in the Philippines consists of a combination of Exempt Securities and Exempt Transactions.

The IRR related to Section 10.1 (k), Subsection 10.1.2.4 of the SRC prescribe the restrictions for Exempt Transactions and stipulate that the following information be provided to potential investors:

  i.   the exact name of the issuer and its predecessor, if any;
  ii.   address of its principal executive offices;
  iii. place of incorporation;
  iv.   exact title and class of the security;
  v.   par or stated value of the security;
  vi.   number of shares or total amount of securities outstanding at the end of the issuer's most recent fiscal year;
  vii. name and address of the transfer agent;
  viii. nature of the issuer's business;
  ix.   nature of products or services offered;
  x.   nature and extent of the issuer's facilities;
  xi.   name of the chief executive officer and members of the board of directors;
  xii. issuer's most recent financial statements for the preceding 2 fiscal years or such period as the issuer (including its predecessor) has been in existence;
  xiii. whether the person offering or selling the securities is affiliated, directly or indirectly, with the issuer;
  xiv. whether the offering is being made directly or indirectly on behalf of the issuer, or any director, officer, or person who owns directly or indirectly more than 10% of the outstanding shares of any equity security of the issuer and, if so, the name of such person; and
  xv.   information required under SRC Rule 10.1.1.

In cases where the issuer is a reporting company under Section 17 of the SRC, a copy of its most recent annual report (SEC Form 17-A) may be used to provide any of the required information.

H. Facility Agent

Under the PDEX Listing and Enrollment Rules (7.3.8), debt securities to be listed or enrolled on PDEx, including bank-issued bonds and commercial paper, must have a facility agent. The issuer needs to appoint the facility agent. The duties of a facility agent include tasks normally associated with a bond trustee or bondholder representative.

The key functions of the facility agent under the PDEx Listing and Enrollment Rules are as follows:

   i.   monitor the compliance of the issuer with all covenants of the issue;
   ii. act on behalf of the holders of securities in the event of any default of the issuer on any of the covenants; and
   iii. regularly report to the holders of the securities and to PDEx any of the following:
         a.   any change, impairment, or removal of deposited collateral;
         b.   acceleration of maturity of the issue;
         c.   any call for redemption;
         d.   noncompliance with sinking fund requirements, if any;
         e.   noncompliance with any covenant or condition of the issuer;
         f.   any event that will affect the obligations of the issuer under the issue; and
         g.   any other action of the issuer or other event that comes to the knowledge of the facility agent that may impair or affect the value of the security or instrument.

The PDEx Rules also stipulate that a facility agent should not have an interest in, or relation to, the issuer in order to be able to act as facility agent for the issuer.

I.   Incentive for Longer-Tenored Issuances

Present tax regulations encourage the issuance of debt instruments (resembling in nature deposit substitutes) with a tenor in excess of 5 years and classified as a long-term deposit or investment certificate in order to achieve a favorable tax consideration for distributions from such debt instruments. In consequence, the market has adopted a practice of issuing bonds in the nature of deposit substitutes with a maturity of at least 5 years and 1 day to provide investors with this concession.

A proposal under Package 4 of the Tax Reform for Acceleration and Inclusion Act references that the tax exemption on the interest income of a long-term deposit or investment certificate with a tenor of more than 5 years be removed and replaced with a uniform final tax of 15% on interest income regardless of the tenor. At the time of compiling these Implementation Guidelines, Package 4 had not yet been approved by the Philippine Congress.

Through August 2019, no bank bonds had been issued with a tenor exceeding 5 years, as bank issuers might want to avoid the complications of having to change fiscal regimes following the expected passage of Package 4 of the Tax Reform for Acceleration and Inclusion Act.

III

AMBIF Bond and Note Issuance Process in the Philippines

This chapter describes the regulatory processes and necessary steps for the issuance of bonds and notes to Qualified Buyers in the Philippines.

A. Overview of the Regulatory Process

1. Regulatory Process by Corporate Issuer Type

The regulatory process for the issuance of bonds and notes to professional investors in the Philippines, typically referred to as QB bonds or Exempt Transactions, has been streamlined by the SEC over the past 2 years. No approvals need to be obtained and a Notice of Exempt Transaction no longer needs to be filed with the SEC. However, the SEC reserves the right to request confirmation of the eligibility of an Exempt Transaction at any time (see also section D.1 in this chapter for a potential, if voluntary, additional process).

With respect to the BSP, the applicable rules and regulations on the onshore issuance of bonds or notes in the domestic market depend on the (i) residency and type of issuer (whether financial or nonfinancial institution), and (ii) denomination of the bonds or notes. A specific regulatory process for bank-issued bonds and commercial paper exists (see section B).

In addition, the listing or enrollment of issued bonds and notes on PDEx is possible in order to allow for visibility and continuous disclosure and pricing (please also refer to Chapter I), and it is required for the trading of bonds and notes. A number of specific prescriptions exist in the PDEx Rules, particularly for the enrollment of bank-issued bonds and commercial paper and Restricted Securities. Details are explained in section B.

Table 5 provides an overview of the regulatory process by issuer type and identifies which regulatory authority or market institution is involved. In order to make the issuance process by issuer type more comparable across ASEAN+3 markets, the table features common issuer type distinctions that are evident in regional markets. Not all markets will distinguish between all such issuer types or prescribe specific approvals.

Table 5: Authorities Involved in the Regulatory Process by Corporate Issuer Type

Type of Corporate Issuer	SEC	BSP	PDEx
Resident issuer[a]			
Resident nonfinancial institution issuing PHP-denominated bonds and notes		X[b]	X
Resident financial institution issuing PHP-denominated bonds and notes[c, d]		X[b, e, f]	X
Resident issuing FCY-denominated debt securities		X[b, e, f]	X
Nonresident issuer			
Nonresident nonfinancial institution issuing PHP-denominated bonds and notes	O[g]	X	X[h]
Nonresident financial institution issuing PHP-denominated bonds and notes	O[g]	X	X[h]
Nonresident issuing FCY-denominated debt securities		X	X[h]

BSP = Bangko Sentral ng Pilipinas, FCY = foreign currency, PDEx = Philippine Dealing & Exchange Corp., PHP = Philippine peso, SEC = Securities and Exchange Commission.
Notes: "X" indicates approval is required. "O" indicates the potential involvement of said regulatory authority.
[a] Prior BSP approval is required for a resident issuance of bonds, notes, and other similar instruments resembling in nature a foreign loan, with public sector involvement either as an issuer or borrower, or a guarantor.
[b] A Monetary Board opinion is required for government domestic borrowing, pursuant to Section 123 of Republic Act No. 7653 (as amended).
[c] BSP-supervised financial institutions may issue bonds and notes, subject to regulations governing the borrowing of banks and quasi-banks under the provisions of the Manual of Regulations.
[d] Resident financial institutions in the Philippines include branches of nonresident financial institutions that fall under the supervision of the BSP.
[e] Regulatory approval is only required for the issuance of unsecured subordinated debt instruments that are considered regulatory capital by banks and quasi-banks.
[f] Banks and quasi-banks need to submit a notification of the impending issuance, together with supporting documents, which the BSP is required to formally acknowledge before the issuer may proceed with the issuance.
[g] Nonresident issuers wishing to use the proceeds from a PHP-denominated bond or an FCY-denominated note may require a policy decision by the SEC.
[h] All matters related to nonresidents should abide by the BSP- and SEC-prescribed framework for nonresidents prior to PDEx approval.
Sources: ABMF SF1, BSP.

2.   Regulatory Process Map—Overview

The regulatory process map shown in Figure 1 is designed to help navigate the applicable regulatory processes in the Philippines that are applied to a proposed bond or note issuance. Individual processes are explained in detail in Section B below.

Figure 1: Regulatory Process Map—Overview

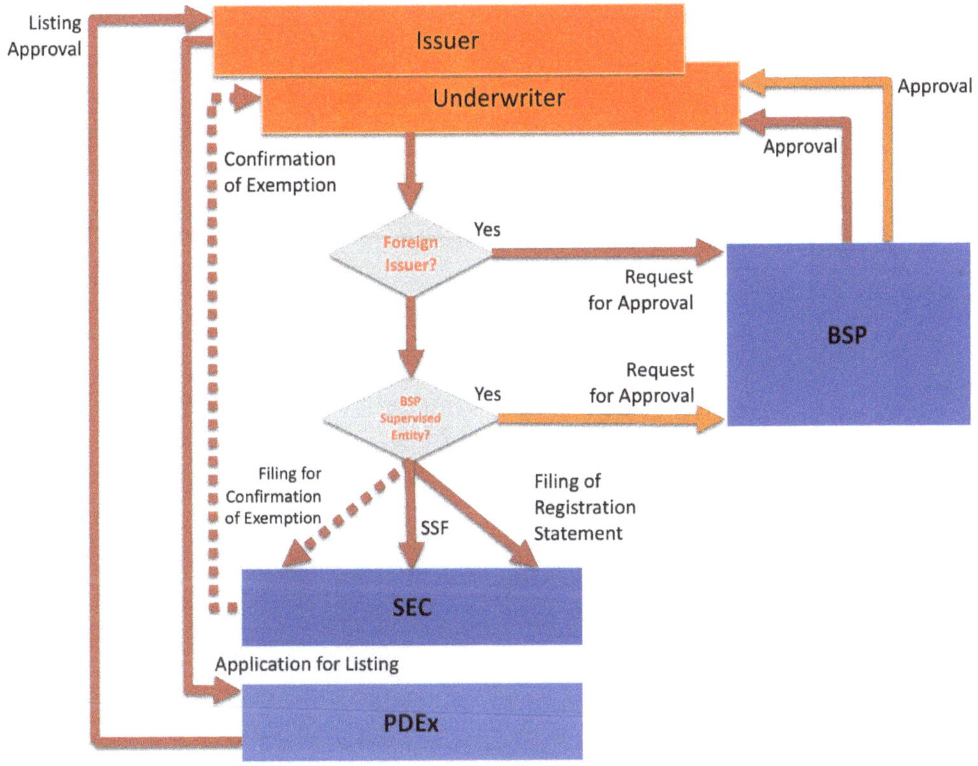

BSP = Bangko Sentral ng Pilipinas, PDEx = Philippine Dealing & Exchange Corp., SEC = Securities and Exchange Commission.
Source: ABMF SF1.

There is no requirement on the use of an underwriter for a bond or note offering to Qualified Buyers. However, if an issuer wants to appoint an underwriter, such underwriter must be licensed by the SEC.

At the same time, typically, the issuer is represented by an underwriter who will file or submit the necessary notification, application for approval, or relevant documentation to the respective regulatory authority and market institution on the issuer's behalf.

B.   Issuance Process for Bonds Denominated in Local Currency

This section describes the onshore issuance process for PHP-denominated bonds and notes aimed at Qualified Buyers, which are known as QB bonds, in the Philippines. In contrast to the requirements for a public offering, the regulatory process for QB bond issuances is fairly streamlined.

Distinctions are made according to the prescribed issuance process for individual corporate issuer types in the Philippines. Sovereign issuers are not covered in this section.

1.   Issuance Process for Resident Issuer (other than Financial Institution)

A resident issuer is defined as a corporate legal entity under the laws of the Philippines. The regulatory process for the issuance of QB bonds by a resident corporate issuer is presented in Figure 2. For the regulatory process for issuances by resident financial institutions, please refer to section B.2.

Figure 2: Regulatory Process—Issuance of QB Bonds by a Resident Issuer

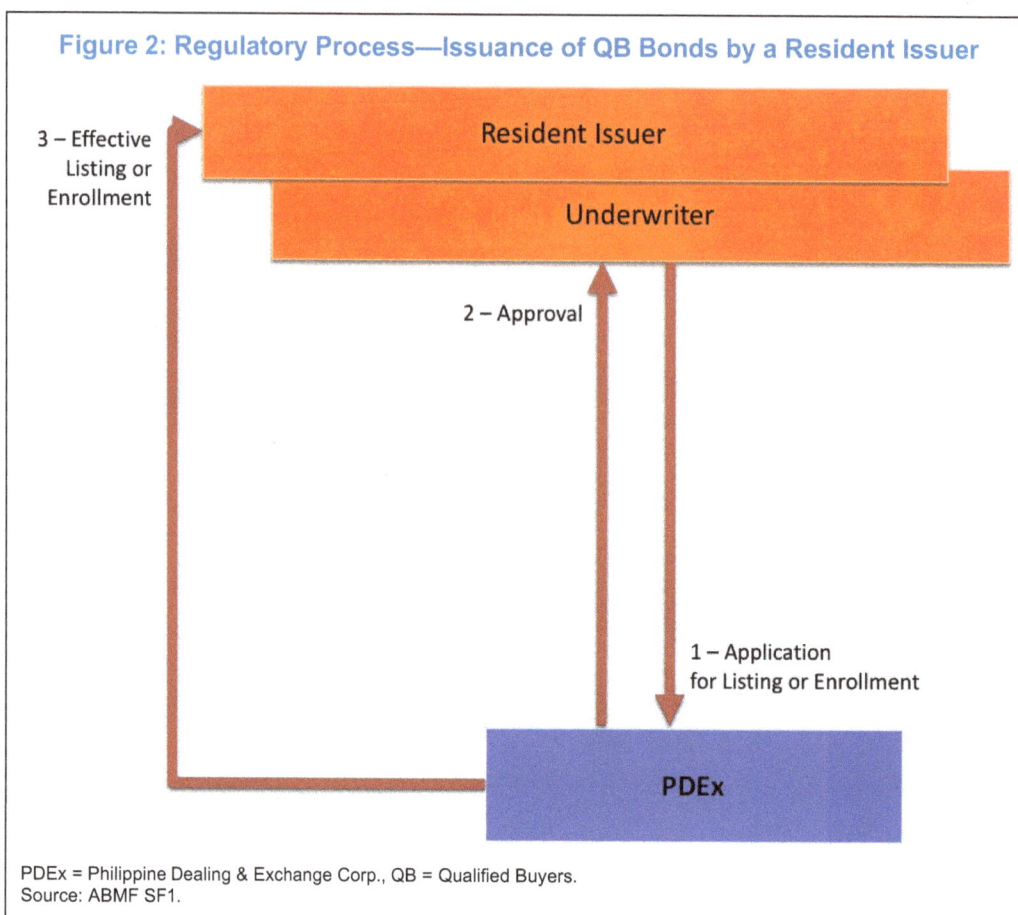

PDEx = Philippine Dealing & Exchange Corp., QB = Qualified Buyers.
Source: ABMF SF1.

The filing of a Notice of Exempt Transaction with the SEC is no longer required when a resident corporate issuer wants to issue bonds or notes to professional investors (QB issuances) in the Philippines.

Since a Notice of Exempt Transaction is no longer required to be filed with the SEC, the issuer has the burden of proof that the bond or note issuance qualifies as an Exempt Transaction under Section 10 of the SRC throughout the lifecycle of the bond or note. Under Section 10 of the SRC and its related IRR (Rule 6.1), the SEC has the right to challenge such exemptions at any time. The SEC also has the right to demand a certification, if necessary. (For more details, please refer to Section D.)

In all offer documents and related correspondence to Qualified Buyers, including the term sheet of a proposed bond or note issue, an issuer must make explicit reference to Section 10.1 (l) of the SRC and give their commitment that said offer is limited to Qualified Buyers, thereby constituting an Exempt Transaction under the law. Please also see the information on the disclosure statement with regard to selling and transfer restrictions provided in Chapter II.D.

To further ensure compliance with the exemption claimed by an issuer under Section 10.1 of the SRC, the SEC also looks to the underwriter—licensed by the SEC—to observe the applicable provisions and selling and transfer restrictions under the law.

The remaining steps to complete the regulatory process are described below.

Step 1—Application for Listing (or Enrollment) on PDEx

The filing of a Notice of Exempt Transaction (formerly SEC Form 10.1) with the SEC is no longer a prerequisite for the application for listing (or enrollment) on PDEx. A corporate issuer or underwriter may now proceed directly to PDEx for the application of listing or enrollment of QB bonds.

For a bond or note to be eligible to be traded in the Philippines, even in the OTC market, the issuer or underwriter of a bond or note aimed at professional investors (Qualified Buyers) will need to list or enroll the bond or note on PDEx. The practice of listing or enrollment is stipulated in the OTC rules by the SEC and regulated in the PDEx Listing and Enrollment Rules.[9] At the same time, trading is not compulsory (e.g., in cases when professional investors buy and hold specific bonds or notes.)

A bond or note aimed at professional investors (Qualified Buyers) will need to be enrolled on PDEx. Enrollment is done by a sponsor, either the issuer or a trading participant. The sponsor is compelled to comply with the obligations to continuously disclose material information as may be specified in applicable SEC rules and regulations and the PDEx Listing and Enrollment Rules. PDEx Rules also require that the issuer appoint a facility agent or trustee for enrolled debt securities (see Chapter II.H for details).

Both listing and enrollment result in the same trading and downstream clearing and settlement processes and practices in the Philippines.

PDEx prescribes that an issuer or trading participant (for enrollment) needs to send to PDEx the application for listing or enrollment as well as the duly executed listing or enrollment agreement, together with documents and disclosure items stipulated in the applicable PDEx listing or enrollment checklist.

The SEC and PDEx have confirmed that the SSF may be used as the key disclosure document in the application for listing or enrollment with PDEx since the SSF was reviewed by the SEC and PDEx, and it contains all relevant information required to support the application, as detailed herein. In fact, PDEx will consider the SSF as the standard disclosure document to be submitted for QB bond issuance after several additional information items have been included in the SSF template. The requested changes are presently under consideration by the AMBIF Documentation Recommendation Board.

PDEx has a checklist for the listing or enrollment of Exempt Securities for resident issuers. The authority to issue and compliance with (BSP and SEC) regulatory requirements for such issuances would be, among others, that which will be requested from the prospective issuer.

For nonresident issuers, the requirements shall rely on and be amended accordingly, based on the framework of the Philippine regulators (SEC and BSP) for domestic PHP-denominated issuances of nonresident issuers of securities. PDEx does not distinguish between nonresident general corporate and nonresident financial institution issuers.

PDEx may, at any time, request additional information or disclosure items from the issuer.

---

[9] PDEx prescriptions regarding listing and enrollment (PDEx Listing and Enrollment Rules) represent Rule 7 of the PDEx Rules for the Fixed Income Securities Market (as amended). The complete PDEx Rules are available at http://www.pds.com.ph/index.html%3Fpage_id=852.html.

Issuers are requested to submit their applications for listing at least 3 weeks before the targeted listing date.

Step 2—Listing Approval from PDEx

PDEx will review the application for listing (enrollment), the listing (enrollment) agreement, and supplementary information. It has a target time frame of responding to the application for listing (enrollment) within 5 business days. The actual review process commences when an issuer or listing applicant starts the submission of the documentary requirements.

If all documents and disclosure items are in order, PDEx will issue an approval letter to the issuer. PDEx may state specific conditions attached to the approval, if necessary.

A fee is payable after the listing; the PDEx schedule of fees for admitting securities applies to both listing and enrollment.

Step 3—Listing Exercise (Effective Listing)

For the listing of debt securities to take effect, PDEx has a target time frame of 3 business days after an approval is issued, on the assumption that no concerns have been identified and the required securities' details are complete and in order.

PDEx Listing Rule 7.6.6 stipulates that PDEx shall announce the admission of new debt securities to its trading participants and the SEC, and publish the announcement on its website. A listing exercise (the term enrollment exercise is not typically used) shall likewise be held to formally and publicly announce the admission for secondary trading on the PDEx Trading Platform and to commence the trading of such debt securities.

The listing exercise is a brief ceremony held prior to the start of the trading day, highlighted by the ringing of a ceremonial bell at 9:00 a.m. by the issuer of the debt securities to mark the start of trading of its newly listed debt securities on the trading platform.

2.   Issuance Process for Resident Bank and Non-Bank Financial Institution

While the SEC is the principal regulatory authority for the securities market, Section 9.1. (e) of the SRC exempts debt securities issued by banks from the need to file a registration statement with the SEC.[10]

If the issuer is a resident financial institution in the Philippines (a BSP-supervised financial institution), the issuance of bonds or notes, including to professional investors (Qualified Buyers) is principally permitted without explicit approval, subject to the regulations on the borrowing of banks or quasi-banks under the Manual of Regulations. However, the BSP will need to approve such an issuance if the bonds or notes relate to the unsecured subordinated debt of a locally incorporated bank, pursuant to Section 126 of the MORB. This particular process is not further explained in this document.

In its Circular No. 1010 (2018), the BSP further clarified the regulatory process for the issuance of bonds and commercial paper by banks and quasi-banks (Figure 3).[11] This

---

[10] SRC Rule 9.1.1 states that the securities issuances of banks and quasi-banks licensed by the BSP are exempt from registration.
[11] BSP Circular No. 1010 (2018) on Additional Requirements for the Issuance of Bonds and Commercial Paper is available at http://www.bsp.gov.ph/regulations/regulations.asp?type=2&id=4013.

section references the process prescribed in BSP Circular No. 1010 (2018). The issuance of unsecured subordinated debt by resident financial institutions is not seen as a typical or likely case for the issuance of AMBIF bonds and, hence, is not further explained here.

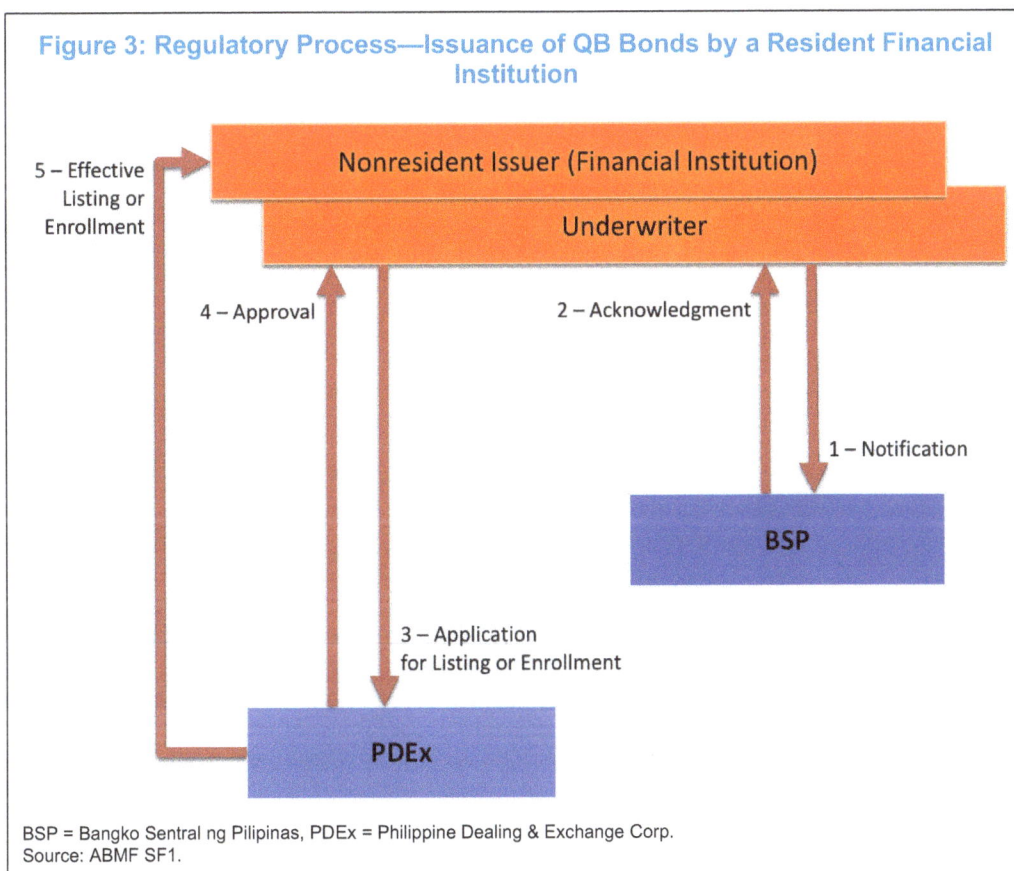

Figure 3: Regulatory Process—Issuance of QB Bonds by a Resident Financial Institution

BSP = Bangko Sentral ng Pilipinas, PDEx = Philippine Dealing & Exchange Corp.
Source: ABMF SF1.

Banks and quasi-banks wishing to issue bonds or commercial paper are required to fulfill a number of prerequisites that are defined in the MORB and the MORNBFI; these prerequisites include audit and supervision ratings, and the resulting actions.

At the same time, the issuing bank or quasi-bank is prohibited from holding its own debt securities and from acting as a market maker for its own debt securities. This includes wholly- or majority-owned subsidiaries, affiliates, and other entities. The holding of such debt securities by the trust department of a bank or quasi-bank for third parties is permitted.

While the issuer has to appoint a facility agent (also referred to as a "registry bank" in the relevant BSP circular), this facility agent must not be affiliated with the issuer, in order to maintain its independence since the facility agent may perform a role akin to a trustee (see also Chapter II.G).

Step 1—Notification to the BSP

The bank or quasi-bank shall comply with the prequalification requirements under Section 111 or Section 41101Q.2 of the MORB and MORNBFI, respectively. The debt securities are also to be listed or enrolled in an organized market (see step 3).

The issuer will have to submit a notification of the proposed issuance of debt securities to the appropriate supervising department within the Financial Supervision Sector of the BSP. This notification has to be submitted within 5 banking days from the approval of the issuance by the issuer's board of directors.

The notification letter signed by the president (or officer of equivalent rank) shall contain the following supporting documents:

i.   the funding plan of the bank or quasi-bank for the next 3 years, including its strategic direction and business model;
ii.   a certification from the board secretary of the bank or quasi-bank on the approval of the issuance of said debt securities;
iii. a certification signed by the president (or officer of equivalent rank) and the chief compliance officer that the bank or quasi-bank has complied with the prudential criteria as provided in Section 246 or Section 4239Q of the MORB and MORNBFI, respectively, and the relevant requirements of the SRC and other pertinent rules and regulations of the SEC; and
iv.   a written undertaking to enroll and/or trade the bonds in a market that is organized in accordance with SEC rules and regulations.

Step 2 Onward—Application for Listing (or Enrollment) on PDEx

Pursuant to BSP Circular No. 1010 (2018), bank-issued bonds and commercial paper require the listing or enrollment of said debt securities at a market organized according to SEC regulations. PDEx is such a market.

Where BSP approval is necessary, obtaining such approval is a prerequisite for the application for listing (or enrollment) on PDEx. In the event that the bank-issued bonds or commercial paper require a notification of the issuer to BSP (see step 1), an authenticated copy of such notification and the certification that the bank or quasi-bank has complied with the prudential criteria as provided in Section 246 or Section 4239Q of the MORB and MORNBFI, respectively, duly received by the BSP, needs to be submitted to PDEx.

The steps for the listing (or enrollment) of a bank-issued bond or commercial paper on PDEx follow the process as described under steps 1, 2, and 3 in section B.1 above.

3.   Issuance Process for Nonresident Issuer (other than Financial Institution)

The process of issuing bonds or notes to professional investors (Qualified Buyers) involves multiple regulatory authorities if the issuer is a nonresident corporate issuer (Figure 4). The regulatory process for nonresident sovereign issuers may differ and is not explained here.

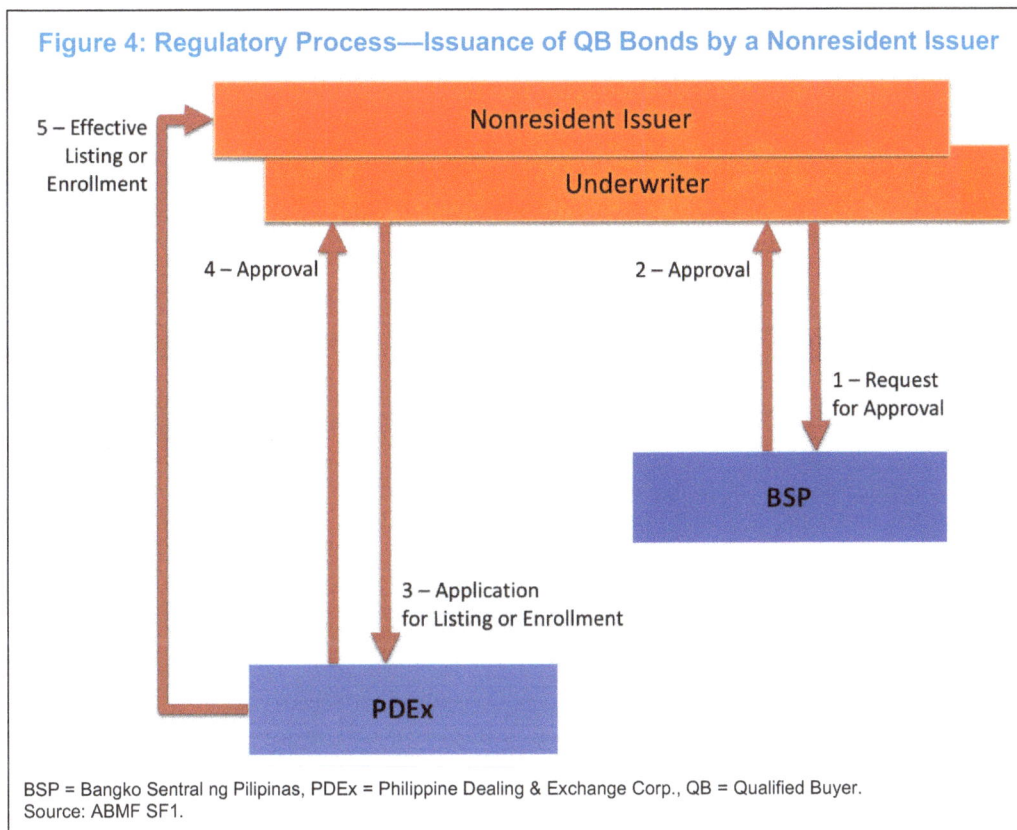

Figure 4: Regulatory Process—Issuance of QB Bonds by a Nonresident Issuer

BSP = Bangko Sentral ng Pilipinas, PDEx = Philippine Dealing & Exchange Corp., QB = Qualified Buyer.
Source: ABMF SF1.

The following steps need to be observed when a nonresident issuer wants to issue bonds or notes to professional investors (Qualified Buyers) in the Philippines.

Nonresident issuers wishing to use the proceeds from a PHP-denominated bond or note may require a policy decision by the SEC.

As agreed among the regulatory authorities, the filing for approval with BSP may be undertaken using the SSF. The nonresident issuer will need to obtain the necessary approval from the BSP before proceeding with the issuance.

The listing or enrollment on PDEx completes this regulatory process.

Step 1—Filing for Approval with the BSP

A nonresident issuer must obtain prior approval from the BSP before issuing bonds or notes in the Philippines. There is no quota or allocation of issuance amounts in Philippine pesos for nonresident issuers.

According to Section 31.3 of the BSP Manual of Regulations for Foreign Exchange Transactions, a bond or note issuance by a nonresident issuer requires the authorization of the BSP—for actions such as the collection of issuance proceeds through underwriters and for activities in the FX or swap markets—whether or not the nonresident issuer will access the banking system in the Philippines. Annex D.2 of the aforementioned manual contains the actual form and data requirements for submission to the BSP.

The nonresident issuer or their underwriter must apply to the BSP International Operations Department using the prescribed forms specified in Annex D.2 of the manual and provide other relevant documents, as may be required, including a

  i.   term sheet;
  ii.   process flow;
  iii. flow chart of fund-raising process, including parties involved; and
  iv.   plan for funding repayments.

The SSF may be used to submit relevant issuance documentation and other information to the BSP. The filing for approval from the BSP is presently conducted by submitting physical forms and documents.

Step 2—Approval from the BSP

The BSP International Operations Department will review the application and relevant documents and may, at its discretion, ask for clarification or additional information.

In its review, the BSP will focus on the purpose of the issuance and use of proceeds, monetary implications of the issuance, any applicable prohibitions, and planned activities in the FX or swap markets resulting from the proceeds or funding of interest and redemption payments.

In the event of an enquiry from an issuer or underwriter on the status of a review, or the regulatory process and other matters in general, the BSP is committed to respond within 15 business days.

Provided that documents are in order, the necessary information has been provided, and the review is satisfactory, the BSP International Operations Department will issue the approval (letter) for the bond or note issuance.

There is no fee charged for this BSP approval process.

Step 3 (Next Step) Onward—Application for Listing (or Enrollment) on PDEx

PDEx has a checklist for the listing or enrollment of Exempt Securities for resident issuers. The authority to issue and the compliance with (BSP and SEC) regulatory requirements for such an issuance is, among others, that which will be requested from the prospective issuer.

The steps for the listing (or enrollment) of a bond or note on PDEx follow the process as described under steps 2, 3, and 4 in section B.1. There is no distinction made between resident and nonresident issuer types at PDEx. Foreign governments and multilateral organizations are also eligible.

4.   Issuance Process for Nonresident Financial Institution

The process for the issuance of bonds or notes to professional investors (Qualified Buyers) by nonresident financial institutions is much the same as for other nonresident issuers described in section B.3 (Figure 5).

Figure 5: Regulatory Process—Issuance of QB Bonds by a Nonresident Financial Institution

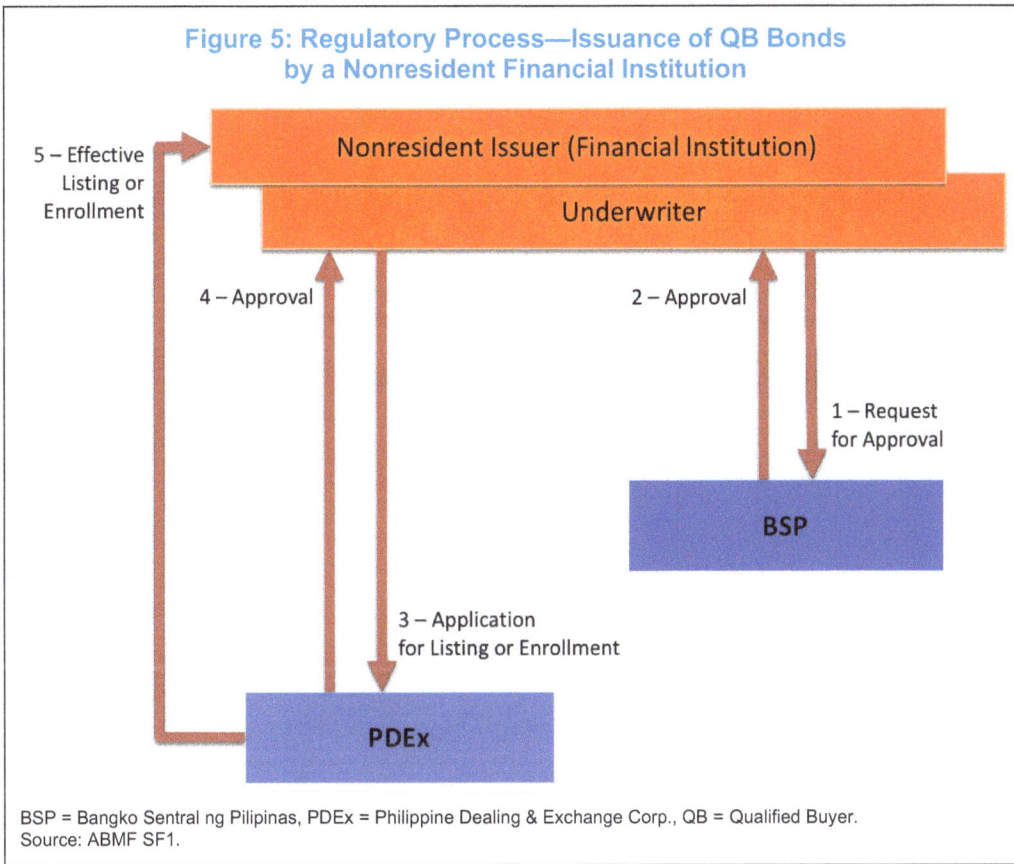

BSP = Bangko Sentral ng Pilipinas, PDEx = Philippine Dealing & Exchange Corp., QB = Qualified Buyer.
Source: ABMF SF1.

The steps described below need to be observed when a nonresident financial institution wants to issue bonds or notes to professional investors (Qualified Buyers) in the Philippines.

Again, the nonresident financial institution may file the request for approval with the BSP using the SSF for the submission of relevant issuance information. Since approval from the SEC is not required, the nonresident issuer must await BSP approval before proceeding with the intended issuance.

While there is no longer a requirement to file a Notice of Exempt Transaction with the SEC, the SEC would typically want to receive specific information from the nonresident financial institution on the use of proceeds, in particular if the proceeds are intended for on-lending in the Philippine financial market.

Step 1—Filing for Approval with the BSP

In principle, the same regulatory process described in section B.3 applies; at the same time, the BSP may apply additional prudence in the review of this filing for approval, in particular with regard to the proposed use of proceeds raised from the bond or note issue.

Step 2—Approval from the BSP

Please refer to the regulatory process described in section B.3.

Step 3 (Next Step) Onward—Application for Listing (or Enrollment) on PDEx

The SEC and PDEx have confirmed that the SSF may be used as the key disclosure document in the application for listing or enrollment with PDEx since the SSF was reviewed by the SEC and PDEx, and it contains all relevant information required to support the application.

PDEx has a checklist for the listing or enrollment of Exempt Securities for resident issuers. The authority to issue and the compliance with (BSP and SEC) regulatory requirements for such issuance would be, among others, that which will be requested from the prospective issuer.

The steps for the listing (or enrollment) of a bond or note on PDEx follow the process as described under steps 1, 2, and 3 in section B.1. PDEx does not distinguish between nonresident general corporate and nonresident financial institution issuers. Foreign governments and multilateral organizations are also eligible.

C.   Issuance Process for Bonds Denominated in Foreign Currency

The issuance of bonds and notes in currencies other than Philippine pesos is possible in the Philippines; for example, a number of USD-denominated bonds and notes have previously been issued by the Government of the Philippines.

1.   Issuance Process for Resident Issuer Issuing FCY-Denominated Bonds and Notes

The following steps must be observed when a resident issuer wants to issue FCY-denominated bonds or notes to professional investors (Qualified Buyers) in the Philippines.

Step 1—Filing for Approval with the BSP

A resident issuer of bonds, notes, or other similar instruments resembling in nature a foreign loan with public sector involvement, either as a borrower or guarantor, must obtain prior approval from the BSP before issuance. Please refer to the approval process in the regulatory process description in section B.3. The governing BSP department is the International Operations Department.

While resident nonfinancial institutions are not required to obtain BSP approval prior to issuance of FCY-denominated bonds and notes, documentation (for bonds and notes not resembling in nature a foreign loan) or registration (for bonds and notes resembling in nature a foreign loan) is required if the FX needed to service redemption and coupon payments to nonresident investors will be sourced from the Philippine banking system.

If the issuer is a resident financial institution in the Philippines (a BSP-supervised financial institution), the issuance of bond or notes, including to professional investors (Qualified Buyers) is permitted without approval, subject to stipulations on the borrowing of banks and quasi-banks under the Manual of Regulations. However, the BSP will need to approve such an issuance if the bonds or notes relate to unsecured subordinated debt that shall be counted as the regulatory capital of a locally incorporated bank or quasi-bank, pursuant to Sections 126 or Subsection 4116Q.2 of the MORB or MORNBFI, respectively. Please refer to the regulatory process in section B.2 for more details.

Please refer to the regulatory process in section B.3 for more details. The review and issuance of the approval is handled by the BSP's International Operations Department. Please also see section B.2 for the regulatory process related to the issuance of unsecured subordinated debt by banks, which is handled by the BSP's Financial Supervision Sector.

The steps for the listing (or enrollment) of a bond or note on PDEx follow the process as described under steps 1, 2, and 3 in section B.1. PDEx, and its settlement and depository agent PDTC, are only able to clear and settle USD-denominated bonds at present.

2. Issuance Process for Nonresident Issuer Issuing FCY-Denominated Bonds and Notes

The regulatory process for nonresident issuers issuing FCY-denominated bonds or notes is principally the same as for nonresident issuers issuing PHP-denominated bonds or notes, given that all relevant regulatory authorities and PDEx (as the market institution) are already involved. For more details, please refer to section B.3.

D. Issuance Process Specific to the Philippines

1. Optional Certification of QB Bond Eligibility from the SEC

This process should be seen as a distinctly separate step in the overall regulatory process for the issuance of bonds or notes since (i) it is an optional regulatory process and (ii) it carries a significant fee.

Filing a Notice of Exempt Transaction is no longer required under the IRR of the SRC, effective 9 November 2015. However, nothing precludes an issuer from requesting a Confirmation of Exempt Transaction from the SEC, which had previously been available under the former IRR.

The function of the certification process is to confirm—to the issuer and underwriter, potential Qualified Buyers, intermediaries, and the market at large—the eligibility of the bonds or notes as an Exempt Transaction under Section 10 of the SRC and the reduced obligations on the issuer and underwriter in terms of initial and continuous disclosure. In such cases, the issuer and/or underwriter no longer carry the burden of proving to stakeholders that the QB bond or note qualifies as such.

The process of certification by the SEC carries a fee, stipulated in Section 10.3 of the SRC, presently calculated as "…one-tenth (1/10) of one percent (1%) of the maximum aggregate price or issued value of the securities".[12] This formula could amount to a substantial expense for the issuer.

The decision to obtain a certification of QB bond status lies with the issuer and/or underwriter, and is not mandatory for an enrollment for listing and trading on PDEx.

The individual regulatory processes for QB bond issuance have been described in sections B and C, according to issuer type and other considerations.

---

[12] Securities and Exchange Commission. Securities Regulation Code. www.sec.gov.ph/laws/srcode.html.

However, the SEC may challenge a claimed exemption at any time and insist on a certification of said exemption, if necessary.

Step 1—Request for Certification of Eligibility of a QB Bond or an Exempt Transaction by the SEC

Any resident or nonresident issuer, regardless of issuer type, may opt to request certification of the eligibility of a bond or note issue as a QB bond or an Exempt Transaction.

The issuer or underwriter will need to file Form 10.1 (Confirmation of Exempt Transaction) with the SEC, indicating on the form the claimed exemption as well as a request for the certification of the stated exemption. A recent sample of SEC Form 10.1 is provided for reference in Appendix 3.[13]

The issuer or its underwriter needs to file five copies of Form 10.1 with the SEC, one of which needs to be manually signed by a duly authorized person who, in case of a juridical person, shall be the president (or officer of equivalent rank) in the jurisdiction of a nonresident issuer.

The SEC charges a significant fee for a request of certification equivalent to 10 basis points on the face value of the bond or note.

Step 2—The SEC Provides Certification of Eligibility of a QB Bond or an Exempt Transaction

The SEC reviews the Confirmation of Exempt Transaction, the corresponding certification request, and any relevant documents. The SEC may, at its discretion, ask for clarification or additional information.

Provided that the Confirmation of Exempt Transaction and corresponding request are in order, the necessary information has been provided, and the review is satisfactory, the SEC will issue a Certification of Exemption for the bond or note issuance to the issuer and/or underwriter.

---

[13] SEC Form 10.1 was amended from the original Notice of Exempt Transaction to its current purpose, Confirmation of Exempt Transaction, effective 9 November 2015. The change of purpose reflects the commitment of the SEC to support a streamlined issuance process for debt securities aimed at Qualified Buyers or other Exempt Transactions.

Appendix 1
Resource Information

For easy reference and access to further information about the topics discussed in the AMBIF Implementation Guidelines for the Philippines—including the relevant policy bodies, regulatory authorities, securities market-related institutions, and the Philippine bond market at large—interested parties are encouraged to utilize the following links (all websites available in English):

ASEAN+3 Multi-Currency Bond Issuance Framework—Single Submission Form
Available from the ABMF website:
http://tinyurl.com/AMBIF-Single-Submission-Form.

ASEAN+3 Bond Market Guide—Philippines (2017)
https://asianbondsonline.adb.org/documents/abmf_phi_bond_market_guide_2017.pdf.

AsianBondsOnline (Asian Development Bank)
https://asianbondsonline.adb.org/economy/?economy=PH.

Bangko Sentral ng Pilipinas
http://www.bsp.gov.ph.

Bangko Sentral ng Pilipinas—New Manual of Regulations for Banks
http://www.bsp.gov.ph/downloads/regulations/MORB/2017_MORB.pdf.

Bangko Sentral ng Pilipinas—Manual of Regulations for Foreign Exchange Transactions
http://www.bsp.gov.ph/downloads/Regulations/MORFXT/MORFXT.pdf.

Bangko Sentral ng Pilipinas—Circular No. 1010 (2018)
http://www.bsp.gov.ph/regulations/regulations.asp?type=2&id=4013.

Philippine Dealing System Holdings Corp.
http://www.pds.com.ph.

Philippine Dealing System Holdings Corp.—PDEx Rules for the Fixed Income Securities Market (as amended)
http://www.pds.com.ph/wp-content/uploads/2018/10/PDEx-Rules-for-the-Fixed-Income-Securities-Market-as-Amended-Revised-29-October-2018.pdf.

Philippine Dealing System Holdings Corp.—PDEx Guidelines
http://www.pds.com.ph/index.html%3Fpage_id=11311.html.

Securities and Exchange Commission of the Philippines
http://www.sec.gov.ph/.

Securities and Exchange Commission of the Philippines—Securities Regulation Code
http://www.sec.gov.ph/wp-content/uploads/2019/02/2019Legislation_RA-8799-Securities-Regulation-Code-2000.pdf.

Securities and Exchange Commission of the Philippines—Implementing Rules and Regulations of the 2015 Securities Regulation Code
http://www.sec.gov.ph/wp-content/uploads/2015/08/2015-SRC-Rules-Published-in-Phil-Star-Manila-Bulletin-October-25-2015.pdf.

Appendix 2
Glossary of Technical Terms

19-lender rule	Prescription in laws and regulations that limit an issuance of debt securities to no more than 19 investors (lenders), in order to fall under Exempt Transactions and thereby allow the issuer to fall outside of quasi-banking regulations
Annex D.2	Annex containing the bond and note issuance approval application in the Manual of Regulations for Foreign Exchange Transactions
corporate note	Market term previously used for private placements in the Philippine bond market
enrollment	Process of listing bonds on PDEx for professional issuances, a prerequisite under Philippine regulations; here, using a sponsor
Exempt Transaction	Debt securities issuance that are not subject to the full disclosure and public offer regulatory framework
facility agent	Financial service provider, specific to the Philippines, acting in the role of an issuing and paying agent, as well as a trustee
filing	Term for action of submitting documentation
Form 10.1	Refers to SEC Form 10.1, which contains the necessary data for the submission of a Confirmation of Exemption to the SEC
Form 17-A	SEC form used to submit an annual report for registered companies
listing	Typically, the action of submitting a bond issue or other securities to an exchange for the purpose of trading, price finding, disclosure, or profiling; in the Philippines, an issuer may list on PDEx
listing applicant	Term used in PDEx regulations for the party requesting the listing (issuer) or enrollment (sponsor)
Manual of Regulations	Key regulations for the activities of BSP-supervised financial institutions; includes separate volumes for institutions and for foreign exchange transactions
organized market	Term used in law and regulations for a market approved by the SEC for the trading of securities, including debt securities
OTC Rules	SEC rules governing the OTC market
PDEx Rules	Short form for the PDEx Fixed Income Securities Market Rules (as amended)
PDEx Guidelines	An extension of the PDEx Rules to clarify the application of regulations to specific segments of issuers or investors

private placement	Issuance method defined in law and regulations for an offer to no more than 30 investors of any kind, with specific prescriptions for advertising and marketing activities
Profile listing	Listing without trading but with specified disclosure
QB bond	Denotes a bond or note issue aimed at Qualified Buyers
Qualified Board	Separate listing board of PDEx for issuances aimed solely at Qualified Buyers (also referred to as the QB Board)
Qualified Buyers	Professional investor concept in the Philippines
quasi-banks	Non-bank financial institutions that carry out quasi-banking activities and, thus, fall under BSP supervision and licensing
registration	Action of registering a bond issue for reference pricing or disclosure purposes
Restricted Issuer	PDEx term for a financial institution without a quasi-banking license that issues Restricted Securities (e.g., subject to the 19-lender rule) or those considered Exempt Transactions
Restricted Securities	PDEx term for debt securities issued by a financial institution without a quasi-banking license as an Exempt Transaction; Restricted Securities may not exceed a maximum of 19 investors during their tenor
sponsor	Party who enrolls a bond or note in PDEx
underwriter	Securities firm licensed by the SEC for the underwriting of securities

Source: ABMF SF1.

Appendix 3
SEC Form 10.1—Sample Format

This sample format of SEC Form 10.1 serves as reference for interested parties. Please see Chapter III.D.1 for a description of the circumstances requiring the use of this form.[14]

_____   _____
Name of issuer whose securities are being offered for sale or sold   Date

SECURITIES AND EXCHANGE COMMISSION

SEC FORM 10.1

CONFIRMATION OF EXEMPT TRANSACTION

[   ]   Application for Commission's confirmation of availability of exemption

1. State the provision of Section 10.1 of the Code under which exemption is based:
_____

2. Information about the securities for which this Notice/Application has been filed:

(a) Title of class of securities being offered for sale/sold	
(b) Form of payment	
(c) Number and price/value of the securities being offered for sale/sold	
(d) Are any of the issuer's securities listed on the Philippine Stock Exchange and, if so, describe which class is listed and latest trading price.	
(e) Are the securities traded on any other trading market and, if so, disclose latest trading price	
(f) Capital structure as of the date prior to this issuance: 1) Authorized capital stock, par value, number of shares and amount	
2) Subscribed capital stock, number of shares and amount	
3) Unissued shares	

SEC Form 10.1 2016

---

[14] The current format of SEC Form 10.1 may be found at https://www.sec.gov.ph/wp-content/uploads/2015/08/2016SECForm10.1.pdf.

3. Additional information about the Issuer and the Securities:

(a) Exact name of issuer as specified in its charter	
(b) Place (province, country or other jurisdiction of incorporation) and date thereof	
(c) SEC Identification Number	
(d) BIR Tax Identification Number	
(e) Address of principal office	
(f) Issuer's telephone number, including area code	
(g) Former name or former address, if any, since filing of last report with the SEC	
(h) Are any of the issuer's securities listed on the Philippine Stock Exchange and, if so, describe which class is listed and latest trading price.	
(i) Other securities registered with the Commission under the Revised Securities Act or the Securities Regulation Code (title of each class, number of shares)	
(j) Describe any other offer for sale/sale of securities by the issuer for the last 12 months for which exemptive relief from registration was claimed under RSA or Section 10.1 of the Code. This should include the basis of exemption, class of securities, amount and number of investors.	
(k) Name of underwriter or selling agent involved in the sale	

4. If securities are being sold by the owner thereof, please disclose:

(a) Name of Selling Owner or Owner's Representative	
(b) Date of acquisition and from whom (issuer, another person)	
(c) Price of securities when acquired	

5. Terms and Conditions of the Sale:

(a) Date and place of initiation of selling efforts (or proposed date and place of sale if prior confirmation is requested)	
(b) Unless being sold by the issuer or the owner, please disclose name of person selling the securities and his authority	
(c) Lock-Up Period	
(d) Summary of other terms and conditions of the sale.	

SEC Form 10.1 2016

6. Information about the Purchaser/Subscriber

☐   Check if purchasers are **existing** stockholders and indicate the number of existing stockholder/s _____.

☐   Check if purchasers are **new** investors not exceeding 19 and indicate the number of new investor/s _____.

(Note: A list containing the information required under this item shall be filed within 30 days from receipt of confirmation of exemption.)

7. Exhibits

In addition to the above information, the applicant hereby submits with this Notice the following documents:

(a)   Written Disclosure to Investors containing the required information under Paragraphs (1) and (iii)(d) *(in case of private placements only)* of SRC Rule 10.1; and

(b)   Copy of other materials to be used/used in connection with the offering for sale or sale.

(c)   If the consideration is other than cash, documents supporting the proper valuation of the payment to be received in exchange of the securities to be issued.

8. Filing Fees

This notice with an application for confirmation of availability of an exemption under SRC Rule 10.1 of the Code has been submitted along with the payment of the prescribed fee in the amount of P_____ under Official Receipt No. _____. *(Fill this up if applicable only)*

Signatures

The undersigned hereby certifies that the exemption applied for hereunder is available and all requirements set forth in SRC Rule 10.1 have been complied with.

Pursuant to the requirements of the Code and SRC Rule 10.1 thereunder_____
(Name of Seller)

has caused this certification to be signed on its behalf by a duly authorized person who, in case of a juridical person, shall be the President thereof.

Date: _____

By: _____
                President

SUBSCRIBED AND SWORN to before me on this_____day of _____at_____
affiant exhibited to me his/her _____ issued on _____on_____.

                                                              NOTARY PUBLIC

Doc No.:_____

Page No._____

Book No._____

Series of 20_____

The applicant shall file with the Commission five (5) copies of this SEC Form 10.1, one of which shall be manually signed by a duly authorized person who, in case of a juridical person, shall be the President.